A DAY AND NIGHT ON A CORAL REEF

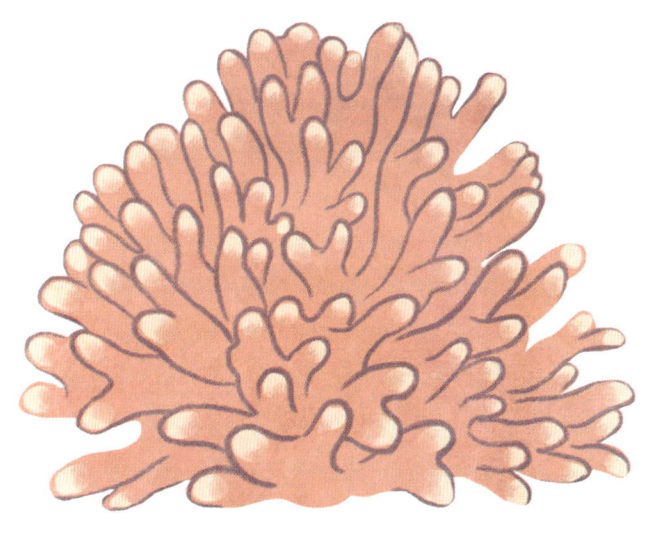

ANITA GANERI AND KHOA LE

W
FRANKLIN WATTS
LONDON·SYDNEY

First published in Great Britain in 2025 by Hodder & Stoughton
Copyright © Hodder & Stoughton Limited, 2025

All rights reserved.

Managing Editor: Victoria Brooker
Designer: Pete Scoulding
Consultant: With thanks to Dr Jörg Wiedenmann, Professor of Biological Oceanography and Head of the Coral Reef Laboratory at the University of Southampton, UK
www.southampton.ac.uk/research/facilities/coral-reef-laboratory

HB ISBN: 978 1 4451 9163 8
PB ISBN: 978 1 4451 9162 1
EBK ISBN: 978 1 4451 9164 5

Printed in China

Franklin Watts
An imprint of
Hachette Children's Group
Part of Hodder & Stoughton
Carmelite House
50 Victoria Embankment
London EC4Y 0DZ

An Hachette UK Company
www.hachette.co.uk
www.hachettechildrens.co.uk

The authorised representative in the EEA
is Hachette Ireland, 8 Castlecourt Centre,
Dublin 15, D15 XTP3, Ireland (email: info@hbgi.ie)

A DAY AND NIGHT ON A CORAL REEF

FRANKLIN WATTS
LONDON • SYDNEY

A coral reef is a crowded place. Thousands of creatures, of all shapes and sizes, depend on the coral for food, shelter and a safe place to lay their eggs.

If all creatures were out and about at the same time, food and space would quickly run out. So they take it in turns between day and night which means there's plenty to go round.

We're going to follow the life of a coral reef and its animals over a day and night to see what happens at the different times.

BUT WHAT IS A CORAL REEF?

A coral reef is made by living sea animals called corals. They consist of many small polyps that look like sea anemones. Their soft, tube-shaped bodies have mouths at the top, fringed with wavy tentacles.

Tiny, plant-like algae live inside the polyps. They use sunlight to make food. That's why reefs need clean, shallow water – to let the light shine through. The algae help feed the polyps and, in return, the polyps give the algae a home.

Here's how a vast coral reef grows:

1) A CORAL STARTS OFF AS A LARVA, SWIMMING IN THE WATER.

2) THE LARVA STICKS ITSELF TO A ROCK AND TURNS INTO A POLYP

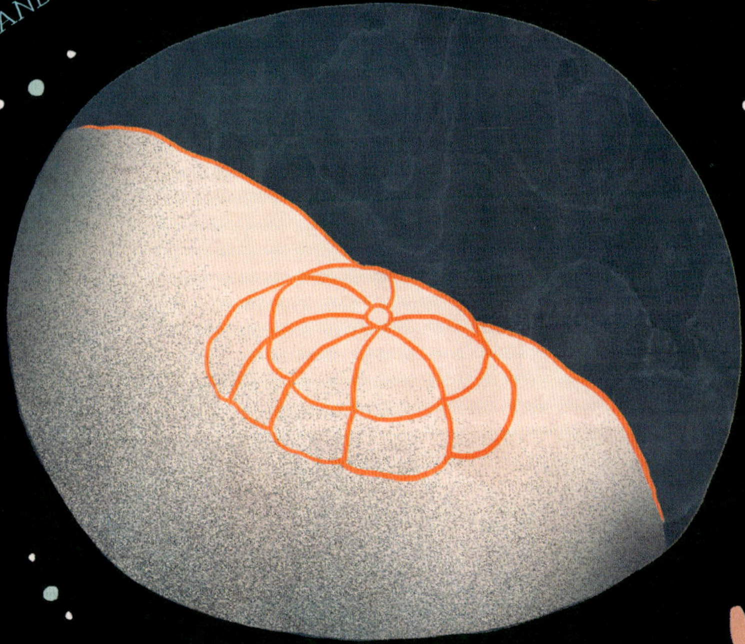

3) THE POLYP DIVIDES TO MAKE MORE POLYPS. HUNDREDS OF THOUSAND OF POLYPS MAKE UP A COLONY.

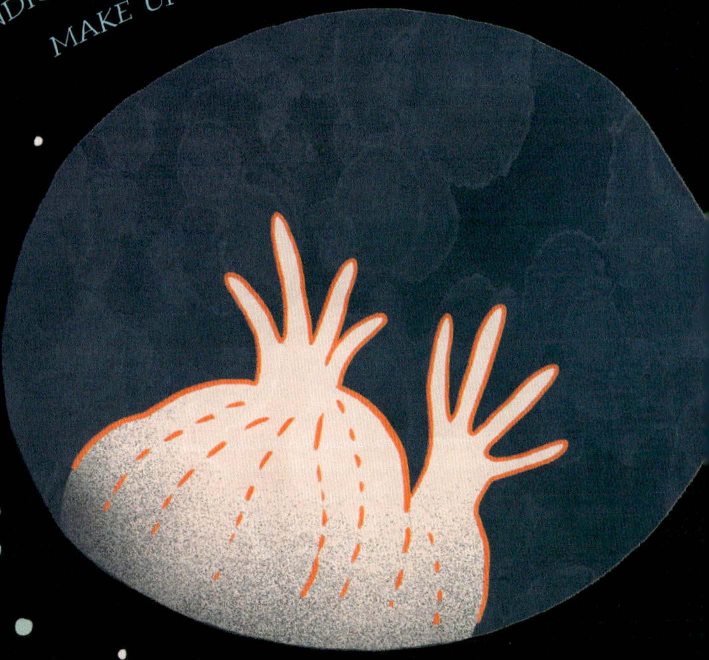

Corals come in many colours. Some of the brownish-beige colours are made by the algae, living inside the corals. Colours such as pink, orange, green and blue are made by the polyps, to protect the algae from too much sunlight.

4) UNDERNEATH THEIR BODY, THE POLYPS BUILD A HARD SKELETON MADE OF CHALKY MATERIAL.

5) EACH POLYP SITS ON TOP OF A SMALL HOLE WHICH IT CAN GO BACK INTO

6) OVER TIME, OLD CORAL SKELETONS BUILD UP UNDER NEW CORAL POLYPS TO BUILD A REEF

It's dawn on the coral reef. As the sun starts to rise, it's all change as the day shift takes over from the night shift. Some creatures, like the reef shark, have spent the night hunting and are ready for a rest.

Others, like the butterflyfish, have been sleeping in cracks between the coral. Animals know when it's time to wake up or sleep by the changing amounts of sunlight reaching the reef.

BUTTERFLYFISH

A polyp's mouth is on top of its body, fringed by wavy tentacles. Some polyps extend their tentacles during the day so the algae inside can make the most of the sunlight. Others extend their tentacles at night to catch tiny bits of food from the water.

With a flash of colour, a shoal of butterflyfish swims by. These fish feed on small sea creatures and algae. Some use their long snouts to pick off coral polyps. Butterflyfish are named after their stunning colours, their body shape – they're thin and flat for fitting through narrow cracks – and their graceful way of moving.

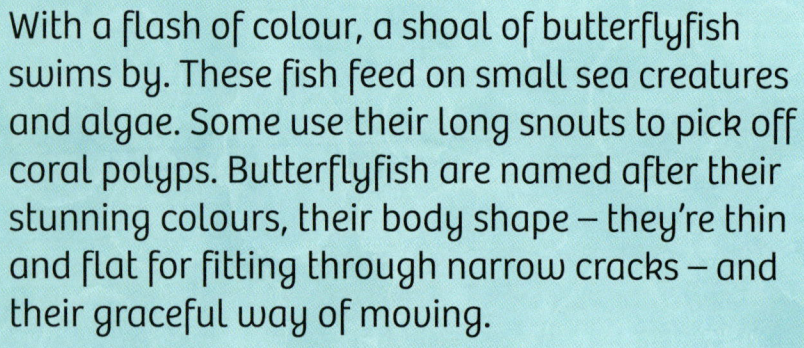

Apart from the butterflyfish, many other daytime fish dazzle or show stunning colour patterns. The colours are used both to stand out and blend in. Fish use colour for camouflage, to signal to each other, to attract mates, or to warn others that they are dangerous. The wrasse turn blue to show that they are ready for their cleaning duties (see page 22).

BLUESTREAK CLEANER WRASSE

THREADFIN BUTTERFLYFISH

Brilliant colours and beak-like mouths give parrotfish their name. They spend the day, biting off chunks of coral, then crushing them up to get at the algae inside. After digesting their meal, the fish poo out streams of sand — it's what's left of the corals' hard skeletons. This is the coral sand found on nearby beaches.

PARROTFISH

Young striped surgeonfish are almost transparent to make it more difficult for bigger fish to hunt them. As they get older, they become yellow with electric blue stripes. Their name comes from the spines under their tails, which are shaped like a surgeon's scalpel. The spines warn other fish away to stay away from the surgeonfishes' patch of reef!

STRIPED SURGEONFISH

For many daytime animals, life on the reef can be risky. They have to be sneaky to avoid being eaten. Nudibranchs, or sea slugs, don't have shells but their soft bodies are brightly coloured. The colours are a warning to hungry fish – the nudibranch is poisonous so STAY AWAY!

Some nudibranchs recycle poisons from the sponges they eat. Others use poisonous stinging capsules from the polyps they feed on to defend themselves. The crown-like structure on their back are gills that they use to breathe.

Stonefish have mottled green-brown skin, covered in lumps and bumps. Sitting on the seabed, they look exactly like harmless rocks ... except that these rocks are lined with vicious spines. If a stonefish feels threatened, it jabs its spines into its attacker and injects venom.

THE VENOM CAUSES PAIN, AND EVEN DEATH!

An orange-spotted filefish loves munching coral. But coral cod love munching orange-spotted filefish. So, the filefish hides from its enemy — by smelling like coral. The cod sniffs coral, not filefish, and leaves the filefish alone.

Phyoplankton are microscopic algae cells that drift in the water. They float in the upper part of the sea where they can get the sunlight they need to make food and grow.

One type of phytoplankton uses its whip-like tail to move through the water. Another kind has a stiffer shape and relies on ocean currents to help it move. For many coral reef animals, such as clams and sponges, phytoplankton is their main source of food.

Half buried in the sand on the seabed lies a giant clam. Once a clam has settled in one place, it stays there for the rest of its life.

In the daytime, the two halves of its huge shell gape open, like a mouth. Its lips contains algae that are closely related to the algae that grow in coral polyps. The brown colours of the clam tissue come from the algae. The bright electric blue and green colours are produced by the clam itself.

The clam opens its shell in the daytime so the algae can use the sunlight for making food. That way, the algae get a place to live, while the clam gets to eat some of the large amounts of food that the algae produce.

At midday, the sun floods the reef with bright light. There is still plenty of activity. Daytime animals look for food, dodge danger and maybe search for mates.

BUTTERFLYFISH SWIM IN SHOALS FOR SAFETY.

A SHARK IS RESTING ON THE SEABED

Because the sun is at its brightest at this time of the day, it is the best chance for a good feast. Algae and other plants use sunlight to make food and grow.

The fish must be careful, though. The light makes them an easy target for hunters. For safety, some fish swim in large groups. Others dart back into their hidey-holes, until any danger has passed.

THE GREEN TURTLE GLIDES UP TO THE SURFACE TO BREATHE AIR.

PARROTFISH FEED ON CORAL AND ALGAE.

THE GIANT CLAM HAS ITS SHELL WIDE OPEN.

Over on another part of the reef, a small group of bright-orange clownfish are hovering around a sea anemone. They dart happily in and out of its stinging tentacles.

If any other fish comes this close, the anemone will sting it and eat it. But the clownfish aren't in any danger. They coat themselves with a slime-like material called mucus that is produced by the anemones so they aren't recognised as food.

In fact, by living side by side, clownfish and anemones help each other to survive. Anemones provide safe places for clownfish to live, and the fish stick closely to their 'home' anemones. For extra safety, they lay their eggs in nests underneath the anemone and out of reach of predators. They also get anemone leftovers to eat, including dead tentacles. In return, clownfish keep anemones clean and healthy by nibbling away at irritating parasites. Anemones also feed on clownfish waste.

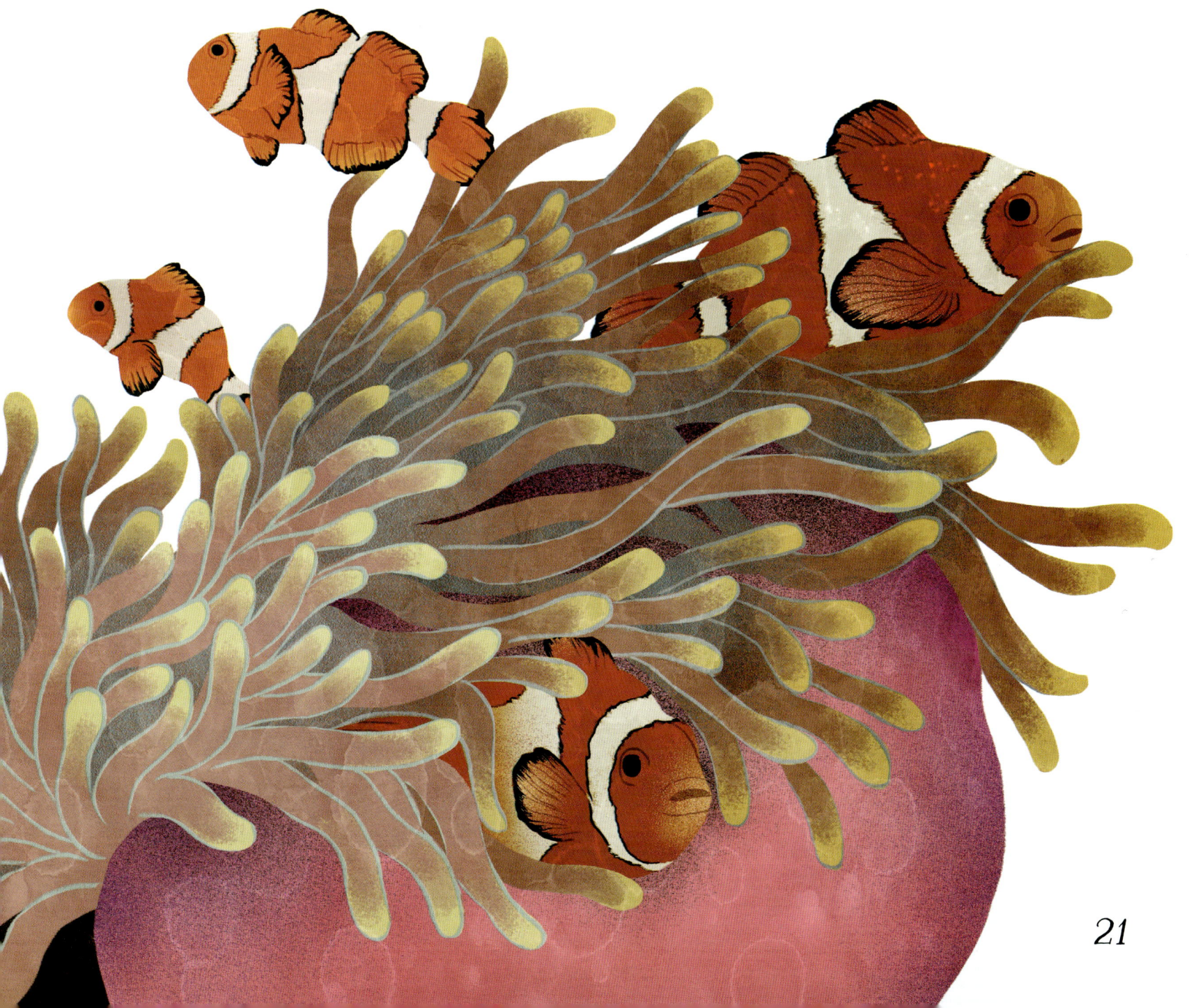

In the late afternoon, it's time for a quick freshen up. All over the reef, large fish, such as manta rays, are queuing up at 'cleaning stations' for their daily makeover.

The stations are run by long, skinny fish, called cleaner wrasse. Compared to their customers, they're tiny and defenceless. But the wrasse aren't in any danger of being eaten. Manta rays feed on plankton, a mix of tiny animals and algae that drift in the water. Other rays live on crabs and mussels.

The manta ray hovers in one place, and waits patiently while the wrasses gets to work. Darting backwards and forwards, the wrasses pick off and eat dead skin and harmful parasites from the rays' bodies. This can take up to an hour, and all the while, the rays stays very still.

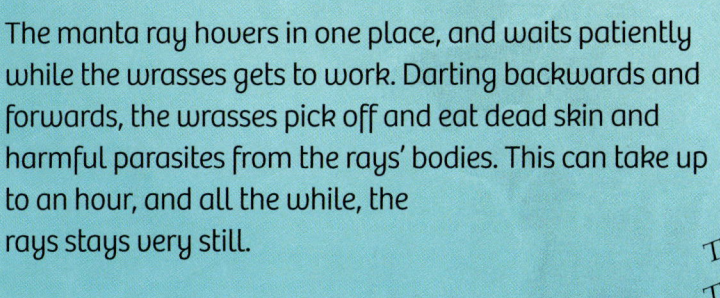

THE RAY MAY EVEN TURN UPSIDE-DOWN TO LET THE WRASSE CLEAN ANY HARD-TO-REACH PLACES.

It's a very popular arrangement. The manta rays stay healthy, while the wrasses get an easy meal. The stations are always busy — a wrasse can clean hundreds of fish in a day — and a happy customer often returns to the same station again and again.

On the coral reef, day is drawing to a close. As the sun sets, it's all change. The reef gets busier, and noisier, as the night shift takes over from the day shift. There's a lot to fit into a short time, though – dusk only lasts for around an hour.

Dusk is when daytime creatures head to their sleeping and hiding places where they will lie low, out of danger, until morning. These may be cracks or holes in the coral reef, under rocks or buried in the sand on the seabed. Sometimes, they are hidey-holes left empty when nighttime creatures are out and about.

THE MORAY EEL LEAVES ITS HIDEY-HOLE, WHERE IT HAS BEEN RESTING ALL DAY, TO LOOK FOR FOOD.

THE PARROTFISH STARTS TO MAKE ITS 'SLEEPING BAG (SEE PAGE 28).

At dusk, billions of tiny animals travel from deep down to the surface of the sea. Towards dawn, they will head back down. It's an incredible journey for creatures that are only as big as grains of rice or even smaller.

The animals are called zooplankton. They float or drift in the water. Some are the young of reef creatures, such as crabs, lobsters, shrimps and jellyfish. The reason for the animals' journey is to find tiny plants, called phytoplankton (see page 14), to eat. It's safer to travel under cover of darkness, when it may be trickier for predators to spot them. Phytoplankton are the first link in the coral reef food chain and in food chains al over the sea. Zooplankton are the second link. After a day spent soaking up sunshine and making their own food, the phytoplankton make a very rich meal.

There are plenty of coral reef creatures wanting to feast on zooplankton. Many rely on them for food. They're eaten by a huge number of animals, from sea squirts and corals, to fish and larger crustaceans. Even though they're so tiny, the reef wouldn't be able to survive without them.

When a parrotfish is ready for bed, it makes its own 'sleeping bag'. It blows a giant bubble of slimy mucus around its body, starting at its head. It takes about an hour to complete.

The bubble stops the parrotfish being nibbled by blood-sucking parasites that attack at night. It also hides the fish's smell from hungry predators, like moray eels. It means that the parrotfish can sleep peacefully in the open, in the middle of the reef.

Parrotfish can feel the vibrations of any approaching predators. If the bubble tears or bursts, the fish will wake up and quickly swim away.

The coral reef is home to hundreds of different kinds of sponges. Their insides resemble sponges that are used in the bath. In fact, the first bath sponges were made from real sea creatures.

Sponges live on top of the reef or inside cracks around corals. Some even drill small caves in the reef for them to live inside. Sponges come in lots of shapes.

A sponge's body is dotted with tiny holes through which it sucks water in. The sponge filters oxygen and food (bacteria and small plankton) from the water. Then it forces the water out again through another opening. A large sponge can process hundreds of litres of water in 24 hours but it is most active at night.

By filtering waste from the water, sponges help to keep the reef healthy and play a vital part in recycling nutrients. For example, the algae partners of corals use the waste nutrients released by sponges. Sponges may not be the best-known creatures on the reef but the reef relies on them to keep it alive and working properly.

On the reef, the darkness provides welcome cover for animals that have been hiding away all day.

Night hunters, like sharks and moray eels, leave their shelters, and set out to look for fish to eat. The moray eel doesn't have very good eyesight, so it uses smell to find its prey instead. When the eel is close enough to victim, it grabs it in its knife-sharp teeth and gobbles it down.

During the day, the polyps of many corals stayed safely tucked inside their skeletons. But at night they expand and turn into predators. They stick out their tentacles to catch zooplankton that's drifting towards the surface. They sting their prey to stun it, then move it into their mouth openings to digest them.

The clam's shell is now partly shuts. At night, it continues to suck in water and feeds on plankton. With all this food at its disposal, both day and night, it's no wonder giant clams grow so big!

Reef fish that are out and about at night have special features for finding food in the dark, and keeping out of the way of predators. Many have large, super-sensitive eyes for seeing in very low light.

Bigscale soldierfish have large, pale red scales and red fins. They spend the day hiding away in caves and under rocky ledges. At night, they head out for a feast of zooplankton. Their large eyes are adapted for seeing in the dark, and they have extra light-sensing cells for making the most of even the tiniest amounts of light.

Flashlight fish, also known as lantern-eye fish, have bioluminescent organs underneath their eyes. These organs contain luminous bacteria that light up. The light of bioluminescent fish can be 'turned off' by the fish using either a dark lid or by being drawn into a pouch. The light is used to communicate, attract prey, and avoid predators.

Famous for its big, blue eyes, the blue-eyed cardinalfish is small and pink, with reddish stripes. For safety, during the day, it rests in the middle of a large, mixed group of fish. At night, it swims among the branches of coral, looking for shrimps and crabs to catch in its large mouth.

A sleek, dark shape cruises silently along the edge of the reef. It's a whitetip reef shark, on the look-out for nighttime prey. This shark isn't a fussy eater and will happily feed on any fish, octopuses, lobsters and crabs it can catch. It's a strong, skilful hunter, often stalking its prey for some time, before suddenly launching a surprise attack.

The bright white tips on their pointed back and tail fins make whitetips easy to recognize. They're medium-sized, beautifully streamlined sharks, able to streak speedily through the water. They have short, blunt snouts and large jaws, filled with razor-sharp teeth. Whitetips hunt alone or in groups, often stopping to squeeze their slender bodies into cracks and holes in the coral so they can flush out sleeping prey. Sometimes, they twist and turn so quickly, they break off chunks of coral and may even damage their own skin and fins.

In some months, female green sea turtles are very busy at night. This turtle finds her way back to the beach where she was born.

Then, under cover of darkness, she swims ashore and digs a deep hole with her flippers. She lays around 100 soft, white, leathery eggs in the hole, and covers them up with sand. Then, she heads back out to sea.

Over the next few months, during the cover of darkness, she'll be back several more times to lay more batches of eggs.

Around two months later, baby turtles will begin to hatch. They'll chip holes in their eggshells, then dig their way out of the nest. They usually hatch at night-time when there are fewer of their predators, such as seabirds, fish and big crabs, around.

It is thought that they find their way to the ocean by using the downward slope of the beach and the reflections of the Moon and stars on the water.

THEY MUST MOVE AS FAST AS THEY CAN TO ESCAPE HUNGRY PREDATORS!

The night is almost over. As the first glimpses of light appear, it's time for nighttime animals to head for shelter, and for daytime animals to take their place. Another cycle of day and night is about to begin on the coral reef.

Over 24 hours, the coral reef is never completely still. From the bustle of activity at dawn and dusk, to the quiet of midday, it is packed with extraordinary animals whose secret to survival is not to get in each other's way.

AMAZING CORAL

Corals grow in lots of different shapes and sizes, and are often brightly coloured. There are hundreds of kinds of coral. Here are just a few – how do you think they got their names?

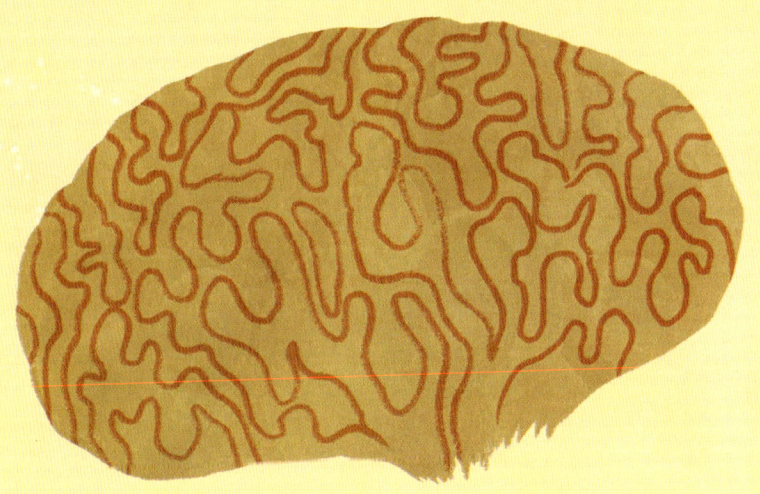

BRAIN CORAL

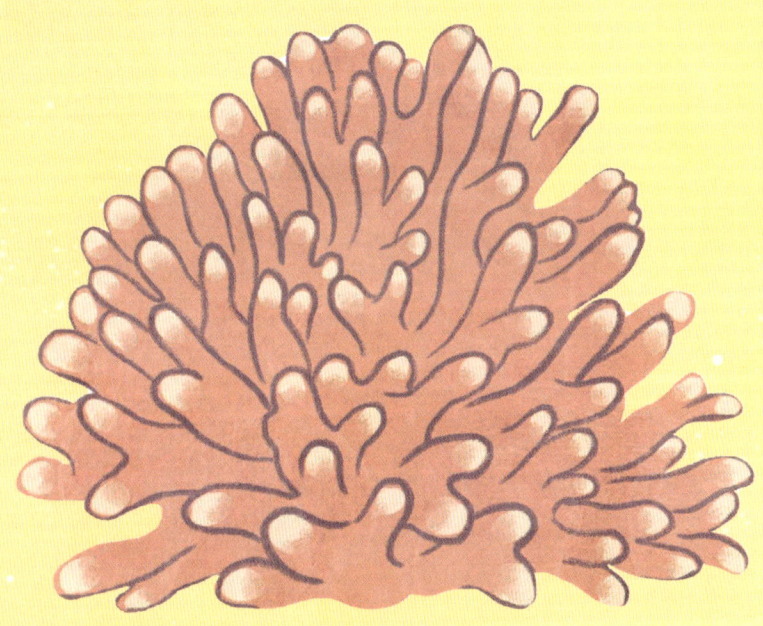

SMOOTH CAULIFLOWER CORAL

FINGER CORAL

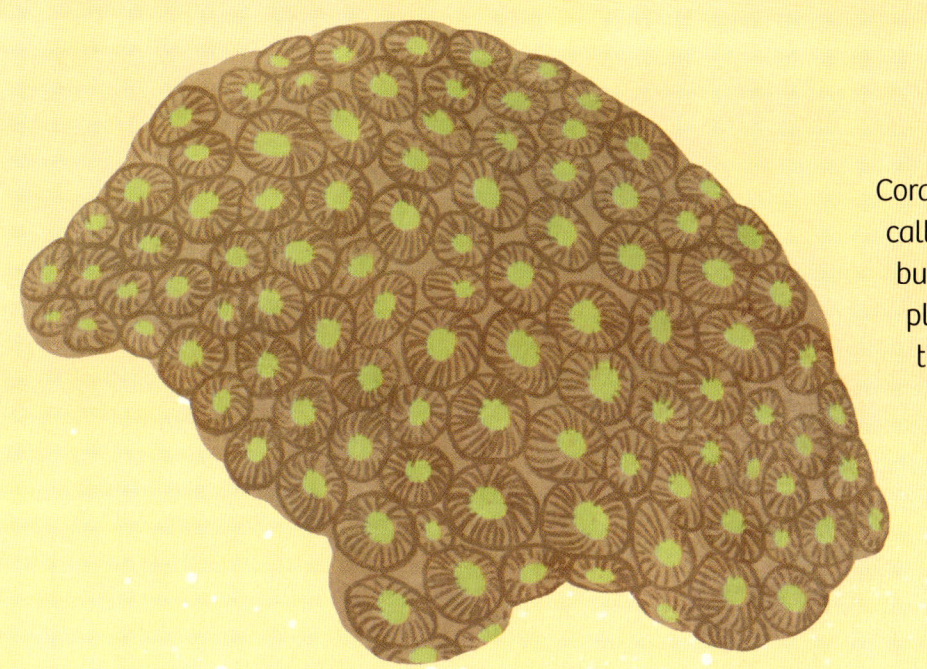

Corals like these ones build the reef and are called 'hard' corals. You also get soft corals but they're soft and bendy and look quite like plants. Instead of hard cases, soft corals have tiny spikes for support.

HONEYCOMB CORAL

COMMON MUSHROOM CORAL

STAGHORN CORAL

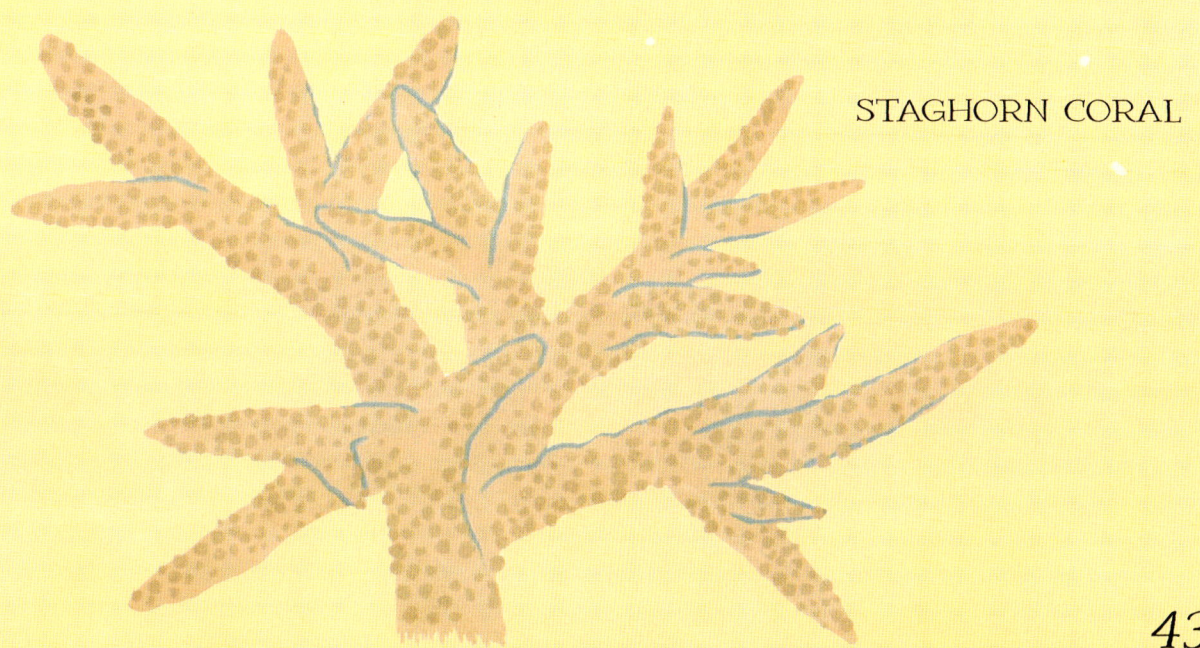

FACTS ABOUT CORAL REEFS

• The first coral reefs formed around 500 million years ago — long before the dinosaurs, and even longer before the first humans.

• Many corals grows very slowly — about 2.5 centimetres a year. That's about the same speed your fingernails grow. The reefs around today are probably 5,000-10,000 years old.

• An atoll is a horseshoe-shaped island that started life as a coral reef, growing on the slopes of a volcano. Over many years, the volcano sank beneath the sea, but the reef kept growing.

• Although coral reefs cover less than 0.1% of the Earth's surface, they are home to around a quarter of all sea life. This includes more than 4,000 different kinds of fish.

• Coral reefs are vital for protecting coasts from flooding and storm damage. They help to slow down waves and water surges so they don't cause as much damage.

- The largest coral reef on Earth is the Great Barrier Reef in Australia. It covers about the same area as 70 million soccer pitches. The largest structure made by living things, it is so big you can even see it from space.

- The Great Barrier Reef isn't just one single reef. It's made up of nearly 3,000 individual reefs, stretching for more than 2,300 kilometres along the coast.

- Today, coral reefs all over the world are in great danger. One of the main threats is coral bleaching, caused by global warming and pollution. As sea temperature rises, algae is driven out of the coral, leaving it a ghostly white. Eventually, the coral dies and the reef collapses.

- More than 1 billion people around the world benefit from healthy reefs for food and incomes. Scientists are also busy developing life-saving medicines from chemicals found in reef plants and animals.

GLOSSARY

algae plant-like living things that don't have leaves but make their own food using sunlight

bacteria microscopic living things in the air, earth, water and on plants and animals. Some can cause disease

bioluminescent when a living thing makes light inside its body, using special chemicals

camouflage colours or patterns that match the surroundings and help an animal to hide

colonies large groups of animals, living together in one place

crustaceans animals, such as crabs, lobsters and shrimps

dawn the time at the beginning of the day when the Sun rises

dusk the time at the end of the day when the Sun sets

larva the young forms of some animals

mottled covered in different colours that don't form a regular pattern

nutrients chemicals that living things need to live and grow

organs parts of an animal's body that do particular jobs

parasites animals or plants that live and feed on other plants and animals

predators animals that catch and eat other animals

scalpel a very sharp knife that surgeons use during operations

shoal a large number of fish swimming in a group

tentacles long, arm-like body parts, used by some animals to catch their food

tissue a group of cells in the body of a plant or animal that work together

transparent something you can see through very clearly.

vibrations lots of quick, shaking movements

FURTHER INFORMATON

Websites

www.barrierreef.org/the-reef/animals
Facts, stats and photographs of the world's largest reef.

www.dcceew.gov.au/about/news/take-a-virtual-tour-great-barrier-reef
Take a thrilling virtual tour of the Great Barrier Reef.

www.nhm.ac.uk/discover/sounds-of-coral-reef.html
Listen to the extraordinary sounds of a real coral reef.

https://coral.org/en/
Find out why coral reefs are in danger, and how to save them.

Books

Inside Info: Taking Apart a Coral Reef by Chris Oxlade and Sean O'Brien, Wayland, 2025
Start Small, Think Big: Tiny Floating Coral by Mary Auld and La Scarlatte, Red Comet Press, 2024

INDEX

algae 6–7, 9–11, 14, 16–17, 19, 22, 31
anemones, sea 6, 20–21

bioluminescence 35
butterflyfish 8, 10, 18, 25

cardinalfish, blue-eyed 35
clams, giant 15–17, 19, 25, 33
clownfish 20–21
cod, coral 13
coral reef
    building a 6–7, 43
    daytime 4–24, 33, 35, 40–41
    nighttime 4, 8–9, 24–41
    providing food 4, 10–13, 19, 37
    providing shelter 4, 8, 13, 18–19, 24–25, 32, 34, 40
corals see polyps, coral
crabs 22, 26, 35–37

eels, moray 24, 28, 32
eggs 4, 21, 25, 38–39

filefish, orange-spotted 13
fish, flashlight 35

mussels 22

nudibranchs 12

parrotfish 11, 19, 24, 28–29
plankton 14–15, 22–23, 30, 33
    phytoplankton 14–15, 26–27
    zooplankton 26–27, 32, 34
polyps, coral 6–7, 9–13, 16, 19, 27, 31–32, 37, 42–43

rays, manta 22–23

sharks 18, 32
    reef 8, 25
    whitetip reef 36–37
slugs, sea 12
soldierfish, bigscale 34
sponges 12, 15, 30–31
stations, cleaning 22–23
stonefish 12
surgeonfish, striped 11

turtles, green 19, 25, 38–39

wrasse, cleaner 10, 22–23

48